Look & Find
SHAPES
to Color

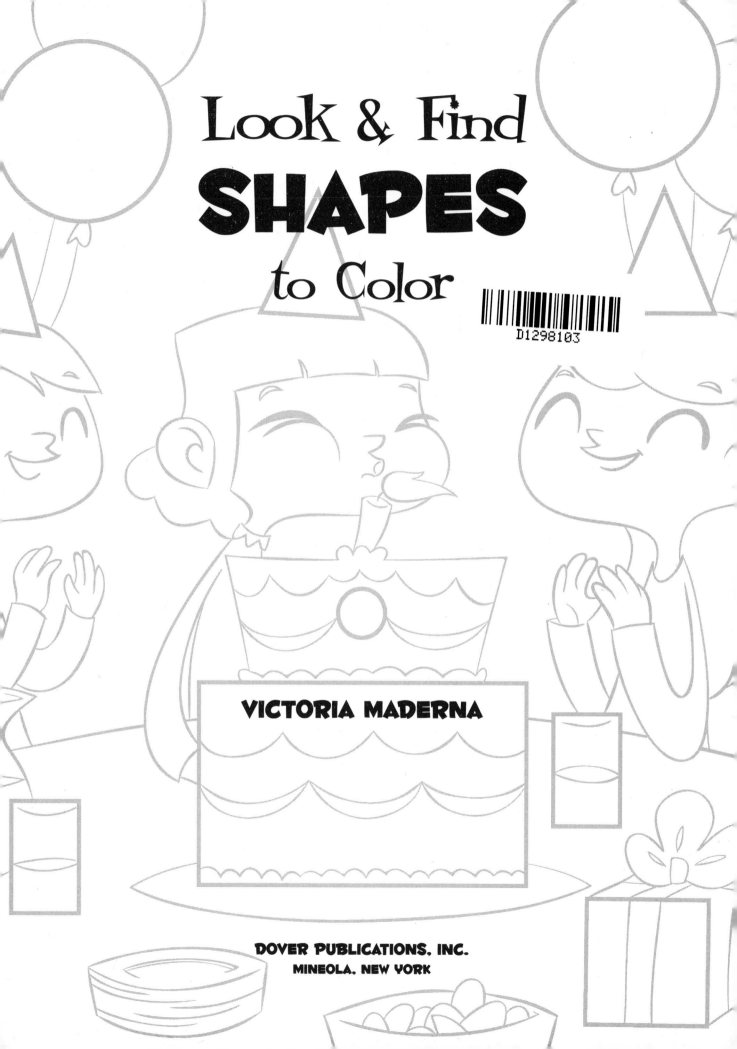

VICTORIA MADERNA

DOVER PUBLICATIONS, INC.
MINEOLA, NEW YORK

GREEN EDITION

At Dover Publications we're committed to producing books in an earth-friendly manner and to helping our customers make greener choices.

Manufacturing books in the United States ensures compliance with strict environmental laws and eliminates the need for international freight shipping, a major contributor to global air pollution. And printing on recycled paper helps minimize our consumption of trees, water and fossil fuels.

The text of this book was printed on paper made with 50% post-consumer waste and the cover was printed on paper made with 10% post-consumer waste. At Dover, we use Environmental Defense's Paper Calculator to measure the benefits of these choices, including: the number of trees saved, gallons of water conserved, as well as air emissions and solid waste eliminated.

Please visit the product page for *Look & Find Shapes to Color* at www.doverpublications.com to see a detailed account of the environmental savings we've achieved over the life of this book.

Bibliographical Note

Look & Find Shapes to Color is a new work, first published by Dover Publications, Inc., in 2011.

International Standard Book Number

ISBN-13: 978-0-486-47991-0
ISBN-10: 0-486-47991-9

Manufactured in the United States by Courier Corporation
47991903
www.doverpublications.com

Can you find 3 circles, 2 triangles and 3 rectangles in this scene?

Can you find 2 circles, 5 triangles and 4 rectangles in this scene?

Can you find 3 circles, 3 triangles and 2 rectangles in this scene?

Can you find 3 circles, 2 triangles and 3 rectangles in this scene?

Can you find 3 circles, 3 triangles and 2 squares in this scene?

Can you find 4 circles, 2 triangles and 3 squares in this scene?

Can you find 2 circles, 5 triangles
and 3 rectangles in this scene?

Can you find 3 circles, 2 triangles and 3 rectangles in this scene?

Can you find 3 circles, 3 triangles and 3 rectangles in this scene?

Can you find 3 circles, 3 triangles, 1 square and 3 rectangles in this scene?

Can you find 3 circles, 2 triangles,
2 squares and 2 rectangles in this scene?

Can you find 3 circles, 2 triangles
and 3 rectangles in this scene?

Can you find 3 circles, 4 triangles and 3 rectangles in this scene?

Can you find 3 circles, 2 triangles
and 3 rectangles in this scene?

Can you find 3 circles, 4 triangles
and 2 rectangles in this scene?

Can you find 1 circle, 3 triangles, 2 squares and 2 rectangles in this scene?

Can you find 3 circles, 2 triangles and 3 rectangles in this scene?

Can you find 3 circles, 3 triangles, 2 squares and 2 rectangles in this scene?

Can you find 3 circles, 2 triangles and 3 rectangles in this scene?

Can you find 3 circles, 3 triangles and 3 squares in this scene?

Can you find 3 circles, 3 triangles and 3 rectangles in this scene?

Can you find 2 circles, 3 triangles
and 3 rectangles in this scene?

Can you find 3 circles, 2 triangles
and 3 rectangles in this scene?

Can you find 3 circles, 3 triangles
and 3 rectangles in this scene?

Can you find 3 circles, 4 triangles
and 3 rectangles in this scene?

Can you find 3 circles, 2 triangles,
2 squares and 3 rectangles in this scene?

Can you find 3 circles, 3 triangles and 3 rectangles in this scene?

Can you find 4 circles, 3 triangles and 2 rectangles in this scene?

Can you find 3 circles, 3 triangles and 2 rectangles in this scene?

Can you find 4 circles, 2 triangles and 3 rectangles in this scene?

Can you find 3 circles, 2 triangles and 4 rectangles in this scene?

Can you find 4 circles, 3 triangles and 3 rectangles in this scene?

Can you find 3 circles, 2 triangles,
1 square and 3 rectangles in this scene?

Can you find 2 circles, 2 triangles, 3 squares and 1 rectangle in this scene?

Can you find 3 circles, 2 triangles
and 3 rectangles in this scene?

Can you find 3 circles, 3 triangles and 3 rectangles in this scene?

Can you find 3 circles, 3 triangles and 3 rectangles in this scene?

Can you find 3 circles, 3 triangles and 2 rectangles in this scene?

Can you find 3 circles, 2 triangles and 3 rectangles in this scene?

Can you find 2 circles, 3 triangles
and 3 rectangles in this scene?

Can you find 2 circles, 3 triangles and 3 rectangles in this scene?

Can you find 5 circles, 3 triangles and 2 squares in this scene?

SOLUTIONS

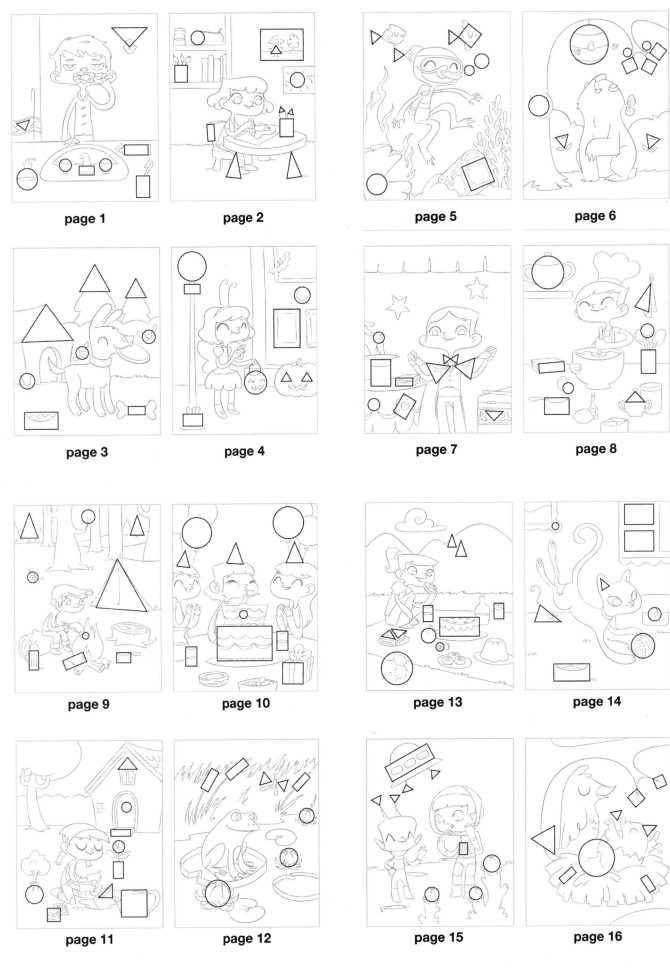

page 1

page 2

page 5

page 6

page 3

page 4

page 7

page 8

page 9

page 10

page 13

page 14

page 11

page 12

page 15

page 16

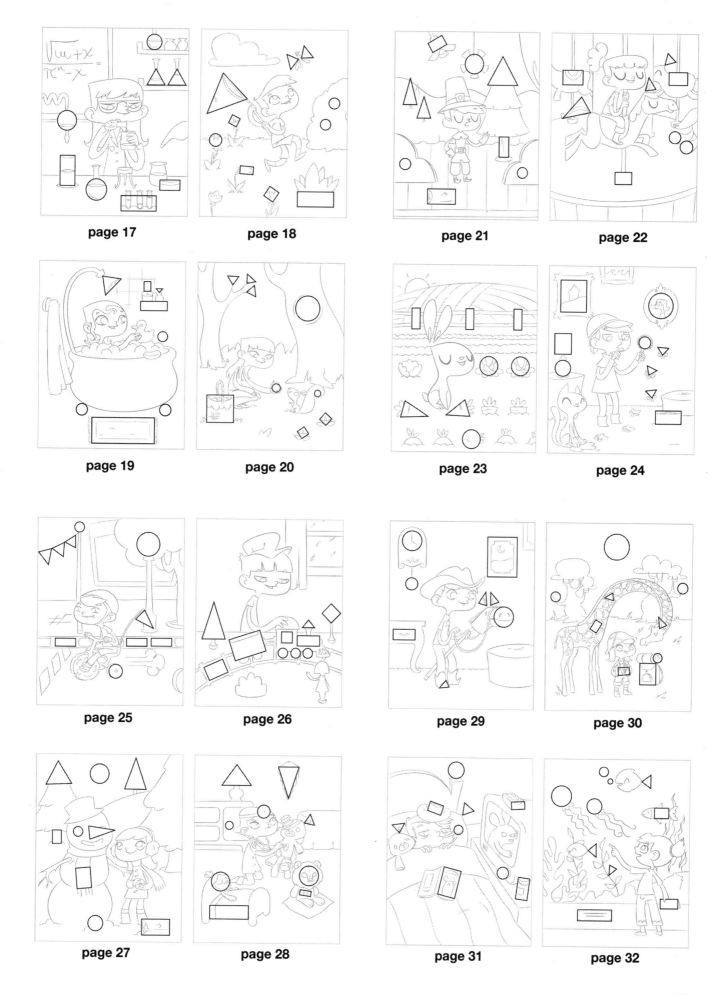

page 17

page 18

page 21

page 22

page 19

page 20

page 23

page 24

page 25

page 26

page 29

page 30

page 27

page 28

page 31

page 32

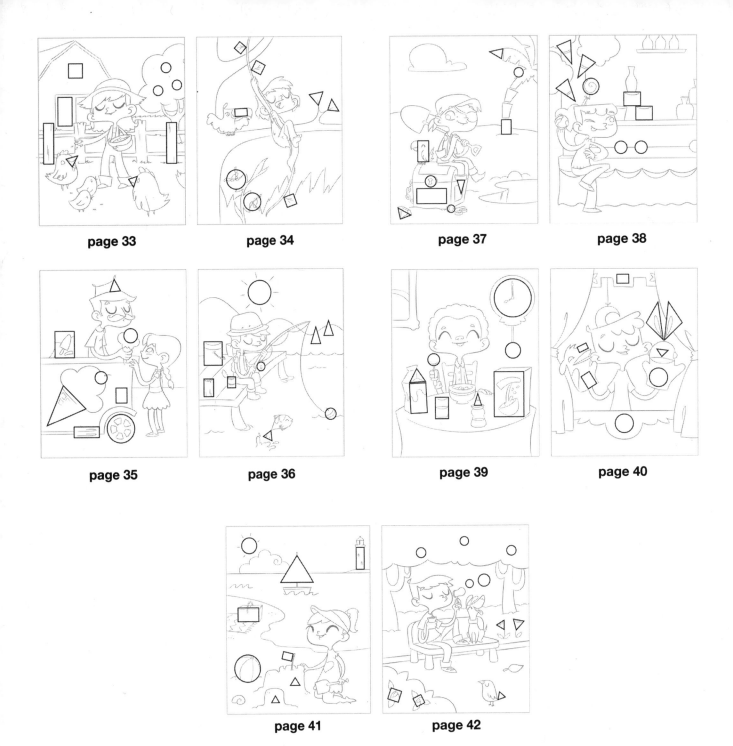

page 33

page 34

page 37

page 38

page 35

page 36

page 39

page 40

page 41

page 42